IRISH CASTLES

P9-DUS-624

IRISH CASTLES

REAL IRELAND

First Published by
Real Ireland Design Limited
1 Duncairn Place, Bray, Co. Wicklow, Ireland.
1988

© Text David Pritchard 1988
Photography by Light Fingers
Design Joe Reynolds
Artwork Shirley Watson
Cover photograph by Hugh Glynn
All rights reserved.
No part of this publication may be reproduced, stored in a retrieval system,
or transmitted in any form or by any means, electronic, mechanical, photocopying,
recording, or otherwise, without prior permission of the copyright owner.

Irish Castles.
ISBN 0 946887 05 5

FOREWORD

Some years ago I lived for a while near Dingle and, having been obsessed with castles since about the age of five, I soon made myself familiar with the few remaining towers on that remote and spectacular peninsula. One day, much to my surprise, I discovered a castle marked on the ordinance survey map of the district which I had not visited, or even heard of, and decided to find this unknown castle and explore it. I ended up in a small farmyard which appeared to be the place indicated on my map, but could show nothing resembling a castle or its ruins. As I stood there confused, the owner of the house came out, followed by one of those snapping black and white dogs that inevitably guard Kerry farms. At first, both hound and master were a little suspicious of me, but when I explained what I was looking for the farmer brought me over to a corner of the yard and showed me three or four flat stones set into the ground. These few fragments, half obscured by a pile of dung, were all that remained of the tower, which had been demolished some years before because it was on the verge of collapse.

Strangely, perhaps, the memory of this anonymous, almost obliterated castle came to my mind when first I was asked to write the text for this book. At the best estimate, well over two and a half thousand castles have existed in Ireland at one time or another and their ruins are still scattered around the countryside in vast numbers. A few of these have survived the centuries with their fabric substantially intact or been carefully restored to their former state in modern times. Others have been blown up, quarried and generally ravaged by the centuries, yet still remain in part and have had their histories recorded and passed down to us. But a large number of castles have been built and lived in and afterwards forgotten, their stones robbed for neighbouring farmhouses and cottages until nothing remains of them but a local tradition of their site, or an untraceable name in an old sixteenth century list. The destruction of the castle has continued well into our century, and it is only in recent decades that much effort has been taken to protect those that have escaped ruination, or attention been given to the important contribution the castle has made to the development of Irish architecture.

No doubt, considering the brutality of life in medieval Ireland, the memory of much cruelty, bloodshed and sheer human misery has passed away with the walls and towers of these lost castles, but with them also much of our heritage as a people has been sacrificed. Nowhere is the history of the Irish as a nation reflected more clearly than in their fortresses and if this book conveys something of the essence of our castles and increases the desire to protect and preserve those that remain, then it will have served its intended purposes.

IRISH CASTLES

During the twelfth century Irish annalists note the building of some
fortified places by Irish chiefs which might have been copies of the
earth castles being erected in contemporary Britain and France, but
the real age of the castle in Ireland starts with the arrival here of
Norman mercenary soldiers from England and Wales in 1169. These
invaders brought with them a system of warfare which had been
evolving in Europe over the previous three hundred years, and had
been tested against the Welsh under conditions that were very
similar to those in Ireland. The value of strategically placed
standpoints had been learnt early by the Normans and from the
very beginning of their Irish incursion they raised castles on the
lands that they occupied. In design, these exactly resembled the
fortresses which they had built in England, France and elsewhere
and were intended to provide protection for the Norman barons
and their followers in their newly conquered territories. Because
the castle was the home of a powerful feudal lord, it had an
important domestic function, and a strong central tower was
placed within the circuit of its walls which could serve both as a

residence for its owner and, should the castle be overwhelmed, a final defence point independent of the rest of the fortifications.

The earliest form of the Norman castle was the 'Motte and Bailey', a type already obsolete elsewhere but ideally suited for the invasion of new lands since it was easily erected from locally available materials and could usually hold off the attacks of forces inexperienced in the techniques of seigecraft. A structure of wood and earth, it consisted of a steep wooden tower on a flat-topped mound, the Motte, adjoined to which was a slightly raised D-shaped or rectangular enclosure, the Bailey, surrounding the fortress. The bailey held the buildings necessary to maintain and house a garrison, whilst the castellan and his family dwelt in their tower on motte. Most Irish motte and baileys date from the forty years following the invasion of 1169, though often they were re-built in stone and inhabited for many centuries. As the stepping stones of the early stages of the conquest their distribution, particularly along the river valleys of Leinster, marks the inland penetration of the Norman invaders from landing places on the east coast. Within the short period of their use a large number were erected and distinctive sugar-bowl mounds, on average about thirty foot high today and now lacking their wooden towers and fences, are still to be seen at many a river crossing or other strategic spot.

The stone castle was a natural progression from the inflammable wooden castle and since it has been in use amongst the Normans from late tenth century, followed the motte and bailey in Ireland very quickly. These early stone fortresses are usually referred to as 'Keep and Curtain' castles because they consist of a central stone tower, the keep (or Donjon as it is sometimes known) with a surrounding stone wall, the Curtain. The use of stone rather than wood allowed a greater degree of sophistication than the Motte and Bailey, but in essence the 'Keep and Curtain' castles continued on the basic principal of surrounding a central strongpoint with an outer line of defence.

The keeps of Ireland belong to the same family as their counterparts elsewhere in northern Europe, though they never reached the vast proportions of the larger English examples and were generally small by European standards. The earliest and most basic type was the square or rectangular keep, which might take the form of a high tower or alternatively be a lower oblong shaped building in which the length of the longer side exceeded the height, although in later years polygonal and round keeps, as at Nenagh Co. Tipperary, were raised in increasing numbers. One other design of keep which should be mentioned was rectangular with drum towers at each corner; this seems to have been an Irish development, first found at Carlow in 1210. Built with considerations of defence very much to the fore, they had massively thick walls and only a few narrow windows, whilst for reasons of safety entrances were placed on an upper level, reached by an external staircase and protected by an outer structure. The lowest floor was given over to store-rooms, and above were two or three storeys which contained the domestic accommodation needed by the lord and his followers.

The keep stood at the heart of the Norman castle, but it was complemented by the walled compound around it. The area surrounded by the outer wall was called the 'Ward', and contained the buildings needed to sustain the castle's various functions of farm, administrative centre and military garrison. Around the ward were the high walls of the curtain, with its towers and gates, and as a final defence a ditch was dug around the castle and filled with water.

The keep and curtain castles described above remained the predominant type in use throughout the first half of the thirteenth century but as time passed and the keep began to diminish in importance, emphasis shifted to the curtain wall and the main gate. In the castles built in the cities of Limerick, Dublin and Kilkenny for example, the keep became merely the largest of a number of powerful drum towers standing at the corners and angles of a four or five sided enclosure with a twin towered entrance gateway. Dublin Castle of course has been utterly changed and rebuilt, but Limerick still has much of its original appearance (although its towers were once much higher) and even at the much renovated castle of Kilkenny the basic plan may still be clearly seen beneath the additions of later centuries.

It is indicative of the early failure of the Irish to defend themselves adequately against the Norman blitzcrieg that within a hundred years they had been subjugated or pushed into the mountains, forests and wastelands of the interior and the Atlantic seaboard. Considering how effectively the castle had been used against them, it is remarkable that the native kings and chieftains did not build more castles themselves, but the Irish chiefs did not willingly accept the Norman system and were for the most part slow to copy its hated castles. During the first two centuries of its existence in Ireland, the castle remained an alien presence on the countryside, as foreign to the native population as the Crusader castles of the Holy Land must have been to the Moslems of Palestine and Lebanon. In these years, the Irish showed more interest in knocking down castles than in building them and it was only after they had overthrown the Norman colony and absorbed many of its elements into their own society, that the castle began to appear in a recognisably Irish form.

Before this happened there was a break in castle building for over a century whilst the Irish destroyed or occupied every castle that they could. From about 1300 onwards, the colony began to disintegrate. Many of the colonists abandoned their homes and fled. Others threw off their allegiance to the English crown and adopted Irish laws and customs, eventually becoming so Gaelicised that they were indistinguishable from their Irish neighbours. By 1400 the area under direct English rule had shrunk so far that only Dublin and its surrounding counties still retained their loyalty to the king. During these chaotic decades very few new castles were built, though there was much revenue expended on repairing the damage done to existing ones by Irish and rebel English armies. Many castles were captured and either became the headquarters of local chieftains or were broken down and destroyed for good. By the beginning of the fifteenth century, however, some measure of prosperity had been restored and there was a great resurgence of castle building in Ireland. English control extended only as far as the confines of the 'Pale', literally a fence surrounding a small area along the Eastern seaboard, and most of the country was under the control of the Norman-descended Butler and Fitzgerald Earls and their allies amongst the Irish chieftaincies. The old Irish Brehon Laws had been re-established over English theories of justice and, even among Norman families, the clan system was becoming the norm for economic and social life. In the absence of any central authority, tribal feuds and civil wars within families became commonplace, with the result that there was an increasing need for personal protection amongst landowners of both English and Irish descent.

The response to this need was the tower-house and bawn castle, which rapidly became the standard dwelling place for the wealthier classes over the greater part of Ireland. Unlike the castles of the Norman colonisation, these little fortresses of the fifteenth and sixteenth centuries were a specifically Irish development. Though paralleled by the peel towers and barmkins of Northern England and the Laird's towers of Scotland, the Irish tower houses evolved independently, so that in appearance and design, they can be distinguished from their counterparts elsewhere in the British Isles. As its name implies, the tower-house was a domestic dwelling in the form of a tower, with living rooms arranged vertically. The bawn was a walled enclosure beside the tower-house, which could accommodate and protect the cattle and lesser retainers of the owner. This type of fortified homestead became so popular that the Elizabethan soldiers and settlers who reconquered the country in the sixteenth century came to see the tower-house as an integral part of Irish society, as worthy of note as the shaggy Irish cloak, or the long fringes of hair that the Gaelic warriors used to conceal their features from their enemies...

'The castles of the nobility consist of four walls; extremely high and thatched with straw; but to tell the truth, they are nothing but square towers, or at least having on more light than there is in a prison. They have little furniture, and cover their rooms with rushes, of

which they make their beds in
summer and straw in winter.'
                    (Mr. Bowillez le Gouz 1664)

The tower-houses were part of a great revival of building activity in fifteenth century Ireland which saw large numbers of churches and friaries built under the patronage of aristocratic families. The Irish age of the tower-house started around 1440 (somewhat later than in Northern England and Scotland) and reached its apogee during the first fifty years of the sixteenth century, declining from that date onwards until the last dateable tower-house still standing, which was built by the O'Madden family at Derryhivenny, Co. Galway, in 1643. The beginnings of the movement into towers may be traced in several areas during the early fifteenth century, where various local factors encouraged the building of new castles and fortalices. The best starting point for the introduction of tower-houses into Ireland, may be found in a law of 1429 which offered a subsidy of ten pounds (a substantial amount at that time) to any 'Liegeman of our lord the king' who would build a tower at least twenty feet long, sixteen feet broad and forty feet high within the counties of the English Pale. The motive behind this statute was to encourage the inhabitants of the area still under English control to provide a system of defence for themselves, since the English government could no longer afford to pay mercenary soldiers to 'ward', or guard, the frontiers of the Pale, which were under constant attack from the Gaelic and English rebels of South Leinster and Ulster. Its effect was to encourage the building of so many towers that by 1449 a limit had to be placed on their number in the border county of Meath. But whilst the government subsidy no doubt stimulated the spread of the tower-house in the eastern parts of Ireland, the ten pound castles were just one manifestation of a trend that was happening throughout the country.

Of equal importance to the popularisation of the tower-house dwelling were the group of exceptionally large towers built around the middle of the fifteenth century by certain of the more powerful Earls and chieftains. These may be differentiated from the general run of tower-houses by their greater size and impressive appearance. It is arguable that they are an Irish manifestation of a fashion for enormous tower-house keeps that was rampant throughout Europe during the later Middle Ages. In England, where the small tower-house dwelling was unknown outside of the northern counties, the fifteenth century saw keep-like residential towers erected at Raglan, Tattershall and Ashby de la Zouche, whilst Scotland also has a number of exceptionally large towers from the same period. In both countries these imitation keeps may be seen as an aspect of the decline of centralised royal authority and the rise of semi-independent robber barons in the provinces.

In Ireland, where the stronger lords had turned their Earldoms and chieftaincies into self contained little Gaelic kingdoms, there are memorable towers at Bunratty, Blarney and elsewhere which are notably bigger than the average tower-houses. Their size and height approximates to the large Norman keep, but they have the ground floor entrance, graceful taper from base to roof, and Irish style battlements, typical of the smaller towers. They are usually found in association with powerful outer defences and might well be described as the capitals of little kings who could raise large armies of Scottish and Irish mercenaries should need arise. Both these larger fortresses and the ten-pound castles provided inspiration for others and from about 1450 onwards lesser tower-houses began to be built in vast numbers throughout Ireland. The slender stone dwellings, which provided security and a measure of local prestige, became so popular that even families of minor importance might possess four or five of them. Well over two thousand tower-houses were built during the fifteenth and sixteenth centuries, with a particularly heavy concentration in Counties Limerick, Clare, Tipperary, Galway and Cork, which between them possess over half the known total. In the still totally Gaelic interior of Ulster and a number of other barren or underpopulated areas (Co. Wicklow, for example) tower-houses remained uncommon, but elsewhere they may be found in sizeable numbers, even as far west as the remote shores of Mayo and West Cork.

In its most basic form the tower-house remained a smallish structure with a rectangular, often almost square, ground plan. For convenience the entrance was at ground level, but the main living apartment would be high up in the tower, often at top floor level so that it could be more safely lit by windows. There would be more small windows and arrow loops piercing the walls of the other floors, but the amount of light that filtered through was limited and the towers were comparatively dark and cold within. Their builders compensated for the lack of roominess by piling in as many storeys as possible, so that tower-houses usually contained five or more floors, with fire places (if they were provided) only on the level which contained the owner's private chamber and in the common room at the top of the building. Invariably towers were vaulted within, usually quite high in the building, but sometimes at ground level, in which case they are sometimes found pierced with 'murder holes', little openings above the entrance passage through which intruders could be shot down. Often secret rooms were built into the haunches of the vaults, so that treasure or fugitives could be concealed if the tower were breached.

Much of the individuality of the Irish tower-house came from its distinctive appearance at roof level. Commonly the parapet around the top of the building was crowned by the three stepped battlements found also in Irish churches of the time, which may have been introduced here from Spain and Southern France by returning pilgrims. Often little square or round turrets, 'bartizans', project from the corners at the top of the tower. The stairs which connected the various floors and the roof might be straight but the most usual form was the winding staircase (Yeats's 'winding, gyring, threadmill of a stair') hollowed out of the corner of the tower nearest the entrance and twisted so that an intruder coming up the stairs would have to attack with his left hand.

If the tower-house was a smaller, domesticated keep, then the bawn was a simplified curtain wall and bailey. Surviving bawns range in size from tiny courtyards to quite large enclosures and it is difficult to generalise about them, especially since so many towers have now lost their bawns. But for the most part they seem to have been only of farmyard size, with fairly low stone walls and not very strong defences, although here and there we find the occasional turret or machiolation at a corner or above the gateway. It is likely that some tower-houses never had bawns of stone, and in the west it was not uncommon for tower-houses to be simply attached to the existing ringforts. Bawns often held small settlements of thatched huts, the homes of the lord's retainers, as at Narrow Water Castle in Down, which in 1570 had 'nine cottages covered with earth within the precinct.' In the sixteenth century the development of better artillery led to bawns being made stronger, and round bastions were placed on one or more of the corners, with apertures through which handguns, and sometimes cannon, could be fired. In the end the low perimeter wall proved to be of greater military value than the tower-house itself, and as late as the last half of the seventeenth century, when fortified dwellings were obsolete, bawns were still built around now undefended houses.

As in the countryside, towers became a standard form of domestic architecture in the towns and cities. Most Irish towns were walled, and important centres like New Ross and Waterford were amongst the most strongly defended cities in the British Isles, but even within town walls merchants built themselves towers that were the same as those in the surrounding rural areas.   An early seventeenth century picture of Carrickfergus shows it to have been a town of tower-houses, interspersed with the thatched cottages of the poorer inhabitants. This is a description of the town of Dingle in 1598...

> 'The houses are very strongly built with
> thick stone walls, and narrow windows
> like unto castles, for as they (the
> inhabitants) confessed, in time of
> trouble, by reason of the wild Irish
> or otherwise, they use their houses
> for their defence as castles.'
>   Edward Wright.

These urban towers, which once comprised the hearts of our towns, have for the most part disappeared, torn down for their sites or quarried for neighbouring buildings. In Galway, once famous for its carved and guilded towers, only Lynch's Castle remains out of the dozens that in Elizabethan times dominated its streets. But in one or two of the lesser towns and villages there are more substantial remains, as at Fethard, Co. Tipperary, which still has several towers in its back lanes and can boast the finest fifteenth century battlements in Ireland on its church tower.

Tower-houses remained the favoured residence of the native Irish and Old English aristocracy until their lands were taken from them and granted to English planters during the late sixteenth and seventeenth centuries. But whilst they were secure, if inconvenient defences, against the minor warfare of Irish society they were untenable against artillery of the soliders of Elizabeth 1. Later tower-houses were provided with pistol and musket loops, but they were indefensible against cannon shot, which could reduce their thick limestone walls to brittle rubbish within a few hours. During the rebellions of the 1580s and 1590s innumerable tower-houses were captured and destroyed, particularly in Munster, and in Munster, and in the following century the Cromwellian and Williamite wars caused further destruction and took a particularly heavy toll on the older Norman castles, many of which were blown up to prevent their being used again after sieges.

As their owners were driven out or abandoned them for more comfortable houses, the castles and towers were for the most part allowed to decay, though here and there, especially in the poverty stricken west, they were sometimes still inhabited and used up till the end of the nineteenth century without any major alterations. If properly built the thick walled, vaulted design of keeps and tower-houses made them exceptionally durable, so that, apart from their thin gables and parapets at roof level their stonework could remain intact for a very long time if not interfered with. Unfortunately they provided a ready source of building materials during an age when stone dwellings were replacing the mud and thatch constructions of earlier centuries in both town and country, so that many were quarried into oblivion. Others were incorporated in later houses and often completely disappeared beneath later masonry, or were simply left in the corners of farmyards and used for barns until they decayed.

Around 1750, at a time when most of the keeps and tower-houses were already decaying ruins, there emerged a new fashion for imitation castles which continued on in various guises into the Victorian era. This took two main forms, firstly the building of new houses in 'antique' styles, and secondly the adaption of existing country houses by adding mock battlements, arrow loops and 'gothic' windows. Even genuine Norman castles and tower-houses were improved in this way, to bring them up to the standards expected by eighteenth and ninetheenth century gentle-men.

Yet despite the ambiguity of their place in Irish history, many enchanting, and sometimes magnificent edifices were raised in sub-Medieval styles. The earliest 'Gothic' castles which came into fashion around 1760 were simply classical houses with trimmings and have something of the appearance of toy castles, but as the century progressed, designs became more sophisticated and cul-minated in superb Georgian castles like Slane in Co. Meath. Many of the leading eighteenth century architects became adept at providing a Gothic 'dress' to their creations and their decorative work is sometimes of surpassingly high quality. The nineteenth century saw the introduction of 'Neo-Tudor' style mansions and then the revivalist movement, which attempted to recreate the Medieval castle, complete with moats and other trappings. At Ashford, Co. Mayo, Sir Arthur Guinness commissioned a huge mock castle, with water gate, turrets and castellated bridge, from the architect James Fuller who had recently completed a similar project at Kylemore in nearby Connemara. In Ulster, work done at Killyleagh, Co. Down popularised the Scottish Baronial style, which became the favoured building media for the industrial potentates of the Presbyterian north east. But the most noteworthy of all revivalist castles in Ireland is undoubtedly at Dromore in Co.

Limerick, which is based on Irish architectural forms rather than on the British and French models usually found in such buildings. Inspired to some extent by the Rock of Cashel, it has a collection of tower-houses, a round tower, Irish style stepped battlements and a detached banqueting hall. Curiously, it seems that its architect Edward Godwin designed Dromore with defence in mind and his mock castle has six feet thick walls to protect its residents. The 'Building News' of 1867, noted the strengh of the fortification...

> 'The corridors are kept on the outer side
> of the building and all the entrances are
> well guarded so that in the event of the
> country being disturbed the inmates of
> Dromore castle might not only feel secure
> themselves, but be able to give protection
> to others.'

Dromore might have been impregnable to the hostility of Fenian rebels but fittingly it eventually fell to that other great Irish enemy, the climate, and had to be vacated because of rising damp.

One of the unhappier side effects of the Victorian mania for castles was that some genuine ruins were spoilt by over restoration and lost much of their original detail. But towards the end of the era, there was genuine resurgence of interest in the tower-house, particularly among the friends of Edward Martyn of Tullira Castle, an important figure in the Celtic revival. In 1916, the poet Yeats, who had been visiting the area for some twenty years, bought the old Burke family castle at Thoor Ballylee Co. Galway, so that he could live near the estates of his friends Martyn and Lady Gregory. The poems he wrote at Thoor Ballylee (published in his collection

'The Tower') overflow with images of the place and its history...

'Before the ruin came, for centuries,
Rough men at arms, cross gartered to the knees
Or shod in irons, climbed the narrow stairs,
And certain men-at-arms there were
Whose images, in the great memory stored,
Come with loud cry and panting breast
To break upon a sleeper's rest
While their great wooden dice beat on the board.'

It was Yeats' original plan to have a stone set beside the door with the following lines written upon it...

'I the poet William Yeats
With old millboards and sea-green slates,
And smithy work from the Gort forge,
Restored this tower for my wife George,
And may these characters remain
When all is ruin once again,'

During the 1930s Yeats lost interest in the place, especially after the death of Lady Gregory, and as he foresaw Thoor Ballylee returned to ruin, but in 1956, the centenary of his birth, Bord Fáilte opened the tower as a Yeats Memorial and museum. Ironically, perhaps, the entrance stone was at last set up as the poet had intended and now stands in front of the tower, which has been restored to the condition in which Yeats knew it.

Thoor Ballylee enjoys a happier history than many Irish castles in this century. The Commission of Public Works has worked valiantly to protect and restore those which have been classified as national monuments, but the sheer numbers of castles to be cared for, the weight of public disinterest and the continuing problems of vandalism have hampered their efforts. Many castles have not been scheduled under the scheme and slowly disintegrate in farmyards or beside country lanes. Fortunately some private individuals and semi-state bodies have become aware of the aesthetic and commercial advantages in restoring old towers and castles, and some fine buildings are now hotels or tourist amenities. In this respect the work done at Bunratty, Co. Clare, must be singled out for praise, since Percy le Clerc's restoration is utterly faithful to the spirit of the Irish tower-house and Aer Rianta have turned the castle and its adjacent Folk Park into a successful commerical venture which is also of great historical interest. There has been noteable restoration at Carrick-on-Suir, where the Elizabethan manor house of Black Tom Butler, Earl of Ormond has been extensively repaired, both inside and out, and may now be admired in its original pristine condition.

Restorations such as these are of great importance, because if properly done they give an insight into the lives of our ancestors and light up the drab pages of our history. Far too many of our castles are already lost to us and it seems inevitable that in due course, others will follow the same path into oblivion. To see a once beautiful edifice like Lea castle in Co. Laois slowly rotting away and being torn apart by the tree roots that are burrowing into its stonework is a tragic and disturbing sight. But every attempt at restoration is a plus mark in the impossible struggle to protect all of our monuments, and one hopes that one day we will at least have perfect examples to show of various types of castles and fortified house that have been erected in Ireland over the last thousand years.

Rathmacknee Castle, Co. Wexford

Dromore Castle, Co. Limerick.

Aughnanure Castle, Co. Galway.

Enniskillen Castle, Co. Fermanagh.

Slane Castle, Co. Meath.

Carrickfergus Castle, Co. Antrim.

Lismore Castle, Co. Waterford.

Kylemore Castle, Co. Galway.

Enniscorthy Castle, Co. Wexford.

Ashford Castle, Co. Mayo.

Malahide Castle, Co. Dublin.

Johnstown Castle, Co. Wexford.

Dunguaire Castle, Co. Galway.

Kilkee Castle, Co. Kildare.

Kilkenny Castle, Co. Kilkenny.

Howth Castle, Co. Dublin.

Lusk Abbey, Co. Dublin.

Gleninagh Castle, Co. Clare.

Bunratty Castle, Co. Clare.

Cahir Castle, Co. Tipperary.

Donegal Castle, Co. Donegal.

Dromoland Castle, Co. Clare.

Mallow Castle, Co. Cork.

Kanturk Castle, Co. Cork.

Nenagh Castle, Co. Tipperary.

Knappogue Castle, Co. Clare.

Doolin, Lisdoonvarna, Co. Clare.

Roche Castle, Co. Louth.

Castle at Lisdoonvarna, Co. Clare.

Tully Castle, Co. Fermanagh.

Leamaneh Castle, Co. Clare.

Trim Castle, Co. Meath.

King John's Castle, Co. Louth.

Green Castle, Co. Down.

Dunluce Castle, Co. Antrim.

Dunboy Castle, West Cork.

Askeaton Castle, Co. Limerick.

Narrow Water Castle, Co. Down.

Blarney Castle, Co. Cork.

Monkstown Castle, Co. Dublin.

Ballyvaughan Castle, Co. Clare.

Adare Castle, Co. Limerick.

Thoor Ballylee, parish of Kiltartan, co. Galway
(was the residence of poet, W. B. Yeats — now Yeats Museum)

Newtown Castle, near Ballyvaughan, Co. Clare.

Castle Matrix, Co. Limerick.

Dunsoghly Castle, near Finglas, Co. Dublin.

Roscommon Castle, Co. Roscommon.

Rockfleet Castle, Co. Mayo.

Slade Castle, Co. Wexford.

Leap Castle, Aghancon, Co. Offaly.

Clonony Castle, Co. Offaly.

Castle at Dalkey, Co. Dublin.

Carrigogunnell Castle, Co. Limerick.

Doe Castle, Co. Donegal.

Rock of Cashel.

Dunmase, Co. Laoise.

City Gates, Drogheda.

Clonantath Castle, Co. Kilkenny, (on the road from Freshford to Urlingford)

Carrickkildavnet Castle, Achill Island, Co. Mayo.
(Grace O'Malley's Castle)

Minard Castle, Dingle, Co. Kerry.

Birr Castle, Co. Offaly.

Oranmore, Co. Galway.

Limerick Castle, Co. Limerick.
(King John's Castle)

Malahide Castle, Co. Dublin.